Who Gets Grandma's Yellow Pie Plate ?™ Workbook

A Guide to Passing on Personal Possessions

UNIVERSITY OF MINNESOTA | EXTENSION

Item #: 06686
ISBN: 1-888440-08-2
Library of Congress Catalog Number: 99-60715

Additional copies of the publication can be ordered from the Extension Store at http://shop.extension.umn.edu/; or place orders at 1-800-876-8636; or email questions to shopextension@umn.edu.

Visit www.yellowpieplate.umn.edu for more information on this and other *Who Gets Grandma's Yellow Pie Plate?™* materials and trainings.

In accordance with the Americans with Disabilities Act, this publication is available in alternative formats upon request. Direct requests to the Extension Store at 1-800-876-8636.

University of Minnesota Extension shall provide equal access and opportunity in its programs, facilities, and employment without regard to race, color, creed, religion, national origin, gender, age, marital status, disability, public assistance status, veteran status, sexual orientation, gender identity, or gender expression.

The information given in this publication is for educational purposes only. Reference to commercial products or trade names is made with the understanding that no discrimination is intended and no endorsement by the University of Minnesota Extension is implied.

 Printed on recycled paper with at least 10 percent postconsumer material.

Table of Contents

Introduction: From Generation to Generation

by Marlene S. Stum, University of Minnesota Extension and Department of Family Social Science

This is no ordinary yellow pie plate. It holds a lot of special memories for my family. It belonged to my great grandmother who spent a lot of time in the kitchen with her daughters baking pies. She gave it to my grandmother.

The tradition of baking pies has continued through the generations and the yellow pie plate is always on the table at family gatherings. Who gets Grandma's yellow pie plate when she dies? My mom does. Some of her favorite memories are of mornings in the kitchen baking rhubarb pies with Grandma.

I hope that someday this yellow pie plate will be mine. It's not just a piece of my past, it's a piece of living history.

— Andrea

Passing on personal possessions is a process that occurs for almost every person in every kind of family. Across the generations, objects have meaning and carry history—for individuals, for groups, for families. Every person and every family is different. The experiences they have when making decisions about who gets what, and why, are also very different.

Today, it is not uncommon for families to be more complex than in generations past. Decisions about property may involve four or more generations, and include spouses, siblings, step-siblings, spouses from remarriages, domestic partners, adopted children, in-laws, friends, loved ones, and others.

The *Who Gets Grandma's Yellow Pie Plate?™ Workbook* is a step-by-step guide to passing on personal possessions. It is designed to be an effective tool for a variety of family groups working to make decisions in different situations. You will find this workbook helpful as you consider inheritance issues following a death or a family crisis, during a move to an apartment or nursing home, as you prepare a will, or when you carry out the wishes of a loved one. There can be powerful messages in who gets what. Planning ahead allows for more choices, the opportunity for communication, and fewer misunderstandings and conflicts.

Regardless of your situation, this workbook is a useful resource for discussing the transfer of non-

> "Objects provide continuity in one's life and across generations."
>
> — Csikszentmihalyi and Rochberg-Halton, 1981

titled property—the passing on of personal property across generations. This is an educational resource that is not intended as a substitute for specific legal advice. As you work with this guide you may want to seek legal counsel. Consult an attorney and your own state laws for advice on wills, intestate transfers, and the legal language and procedures to formalize your decisions about the transfer of personal possessions.

Helping Families Through Education

This workbook was developed by University of Minnesota Extension and the Department of Family Social Science, who have long been dedicated to issues that affect the health and well being of families. We recognize that people have difficulty finding useful information about the inheritance of personal property—items such as photographs, coin collections, guns and dishes. It is not uncommon for such items to have greater sentimental value than monetary value. Consequently, they are often overlooked in the process of drafting a will or planning for a life change.

This workbook provides families with the information they need to make decisions and improve personal relationships as they work through what can be a challenging and emotional process. The *Who Gets Grandma's Yellow Pie Plate?™* educational tools, like this workbook and resources found online at www.yellowpieplate.umn.edu, are the result of extensive research, development and teaching. This information reflects the real-life experiences of families, attorneys and educators. It will help you and your family discuss and make decisions about passing on personal possessions.

Chapter 1: Who Gets Grandma's Yellow Pie Plate? Families and Personal Property Inheritance

by Marlene S. Stum, University of Minnesota Extension and Department of Family Social Science

Recently, my parents died within three months of each other. My sister, brother and I have been going through the house, making decisions about who gets what. It's gone pretty smoothly.

There is only one item in the whole house that all three of us would really like to have: the Winnie-the-Pooh book that Mom read to us when we were young. It was always kept in the corner bookshelf in the living room.

For now we've decided it will stay on the bookshelf, because my brother is moving into the house, and we can't figure out a fair way to decide who gets it.

— Julia

The Issue That Affects Everyone

Almost everyone has personal belongings such as wedding photographs, a baseball glove, or a yellow pie plate that contain meaning for them and for other members of their family. What happens to your personal belongings when you die? Who decides who gets what? How can decisions be made during one's lifetime? Planning for the transfer of such items is a challenge facing owners and, potentially, family members and legal representatives who may be left to make decisions when a family member dies.

Today's families vary widely. People are living longer and tend to experience more transitions in their lifetime than previous generations. For example, they may move in and out of marriage, or remarry late in life. They may form lifelong bonds with close friends, or with the children of friends. It is not uncommon for children, grandchildren, and even great grandchildren to be affected by the decisions of the property owner.

Your family situation and the timing of your decisions will influence your priorities, goals and choices as you work through this process. Perhaps you are the property owner and you are expecting to move to a new home. Your goals

People you think of as family may not be defined as family according to inheritance law in your state.

may differ from those of a personal representative (estate executor) whose parent has just died. An adult child of aging parents may have different priorities from those of a single person or childless couple. The choices considered by a person with a terminal illness may not be the same as those considered by a couple remarrying later in life and combining two households. Because it is natural for the goals, priorities and choices of people in the same family to differ, it is recommended that you answer questions and complete worksheets based on your own, personal feelings and opinions.

It is also important to note at this point that people you think of as family may not be defined as family according to inheritance law in your state. Do you have stepchildren? Do you have children born out of wedlock? If so, do you know what you need to do legally to be sure they are included? Did you know that, in some states if you die without a will, your spouse may legally inherit all your possessions? This means that if you have adult children from a previous marriage they may not inherit unless you've specifically included them in legal documents. Perhaps you have a close friend to whom you've promised a special keepsake. Does anyone in your family know this? Do you have pets? Have you talked with anyone about caring for them when you become unable to? Because inheritance law differs in each state, it is important to explore questions such as these and to take steps to ensure that your wishes are clearly understood.

Who gets personal property is an issue frequently ignored until a crisis occurs. It is often assumed to be an unimportant issue or an issue that will take care of itself. Experiences of family members and their attorneys suggest otherwise. The transfer of non-titled property is an issue that impacts individuals regardless of their financial worth, heritage or cultural background. It is an issue that affects everyone.

Decisions About Both Titled and Non-titled Property are Important

Paring down and transferring personal property are inevitable when owners move or die. Few individuals plan ahead regarding who should get what of their personal belongings. Personal belongings such as jewelry, stamp collections, a microwave, or sports equipment are referred to as "non-titled property." This means there is no legal document (such as a title) to indicate who officially owns the item.

Non-titled property may or may not have a great deal of financial value, but often has a great deal of sentimental or emotional value. Many people are familiar with the need to make decisions prior to their death about what happens to their home, savings accounts, vehicles or other property that has a title. A will is an example of a legal tool used to indicate preferences about who gets what titled property when the owner dies. In many cases, however, individuals fail to plan ahead to include non-titled property as part of this decision-making process.

What surprises many people is that the transfer of non-titled personal property can create more challenges among family members than the transfer of titled property.

Definition

Non-titled Property:

Non-titled property is a term referring to personal items without a legal document (such as a title) to indicate who officially owns the item. These personal possessions may have monetary worth, or they may be cherished primarily for their sentimental value. Non-titled property can include items such as:

Furniture

Dishes

Collections

Sporting equipment

Photographs

Printed items

Family documents

Linens and needlework

Musical instruments

Guns

Jewelry

Tools

Pets

Toys

Non-titled personal property transfers may offer these challenges:

* Personal belongings have different meanings for each individual;
* It is often the sentimental value or meaning attached to the personal property that is important, not the financial or dollar value;
* It is often very difficult to divide items with sentimental value in a way considered fair to all parties;
* People commonly have different perceptions of what constitutes a fair process and fair results;
* Talking about one's possessions is much more personal than talking about financial assets. It often means facing one's own death as well as the death of family members.

Factors to Consider in this Process

There are no magic formulas or solutions available for transferring personal property. There are, however, some factors to consider whether you are planning for the transfer of your own personal property or working with family members or legal representatives to plan for the transfer of property of a family member who has died. *Who Gets Grandma's Yellow Pie Plate?™* materials, like this workbook and resources found online at www.yellowpieplate.umn.edu, contain information and tools to help family members transfer personal property. Transferring personal property can be a way to continue traditions and family history. It can be a time to share memories and stories, and to celebrate a person's life.

You are already taking an important step. By reading the *Who Gets Grandma's Yellow Pie Plate?™ Workbook* you are beginning a practical, action-oriented process to guide you in transferring personal possessions from person to person, from generation to generation.

Research has identified <u>six primary factors to consider</u> in this process. The information, stories, worksheets and other tools in this book will guide you through these factors. Consider these factors:

1. <u>Understand the sensitivity of the issue of transferring personal property;</u>

2. <u>Determine what you want to accomplish in the transfer;</u>

3. <u>Decide what is "fair" in the context of your family;</u>

4. <u>Understand that belongings have different meanings for different individuals;</u>

5. <u>Consider distribution options and consequences; and</u>

6. <u>Agree to manage conflicts if they arise.</u>

Why are you interested in getting more guidance in passing on personal possessions? "Worksheet 1: My Reasons for Completing this Workbook" will help you identify your reasons.

The best legacy you can give your loved ones is that of positive relationships with their siblings, relatives and friends.

Worksheet 1 My Reasons for Completing this Workbook

Name: _____ Date: _____

Directions: Read each item and check off those that are important to you. Add other items as needed. Complete this list on your own before sharing with others.

I want to:

☐ Maintain harmony within my family.

☐ Give myself peace of mind.

☐ Initiate a difficult, but inevitable discussion in a less stressful manner.

☐ Explore my goals and what I want to accomplish.

☐ Understand the goals of others.

☐ Decide what I think is a fair way to make these decisions.

☐ Discover what my family thinks is a fair way to make decisions.

☐ Determine who will be involved in making the decisions.

☐ Learn what items are important to family members.

☐ Tell others why personal items have value to me.

☐ Record personal and family history surrounding important keepsakes.

☐ Learn strategies (and their consequences) for passing on belongings.

☐ Decide on ground rules before beginning the transfer process.

☐ Learn how to manage conflicts if they arise.

☐ Learn how to put my plan into action after decisions have been made.

☐ Other:

Worksheet 1: My Reasons for Completing this Workbook (cont.)

What Did You Learn?

Go back and review your reasons for completing this workbook. Of the reasons you checked, which do you consider the most important? List them below.

1

2

3

This worksheet was written by Marlene S. Stum, University of Minnesota Extension and Department of Family Social Science.

In accordance with the Americans with Disabilities Act, this worksheet is available in alternative formats upon request. Direct requests to 1-800-876-8636.

University of Minnesota Extension is an equal opportunity educator and employer.

Visit us online at www.yellowpieplate.umn.edu.

▶ Next Steps

Now that you understand your reasons for completing this guide, it is time to learn why decisions about personal property can be emotional, and why who gets what can carry such powerful messages. You're also ready to begin the conversation about passing on personal possessions with family members and loved ones. This information is covered in "Chapter 2: Understanding the Sensitivity of Transferring Personal Property."

Notes:

Chapter 2: Understand the Sensitivity of Transferring Personal Property

by Marlene S. Stum and Christy Bubolz, University of Minnesota Extension

When Mom went into the nursing home, the family disagreed about family possessions that were put in temporary storage, especially a third-generation organ. Mom has Alzheimer's disease and wasn't able to make decisions about who should get what. She never put anything into writing.

Four of us siblings think we should divide up the property now, while two think it's very disrespectful to even think about such a thing while Mom is still alive. I think they just can't face the fact that Mom will die someday. In the meantime, the organ is deteriorating in storage, when I could be caring for it and enjoying it.

— Rachel

It's Only a Pie Plate, Right?

Decisions about who gets what non-titled personal property may appear minor and easy. In reality, decisions about personal property can be extremely difficult and become major challenges for family members. The issue is frequently avoided, usually because it is too sensitive or doesn't seem urgent. This chapter will help you understand why transferring non-titled property can be a sensitive issue. Strategies for dealing with the sensitivity are suggested to ease the transfer process and help minimize conflicts among family members. Information is included about how to bring up the topic, tips for talking about it, and reasons frequently given for avoiding it.

While Grandma's yellow pie plate or Dad's hat collection are simply material possessions, such personal belongings can trigger memories and feelings. It is important to recognize the sentimental value that property may have for both owners and receivers. It's also critical to recognize that, for others, such items may not carry much meaning and indeed may be just "stuff." Decisions about personal property involve dealing with the emotions connected to objects accumulated over a lifetime or across generations. It is often the emotional value attached to personal belongings that makes non-titled property transfers challenging.

Who Gets Grandma's Yellow Pie Plate?™ Workbook

Sensitivity 11

Decisions about personal property can be extremely difficult.

Facing Loss and Transitions

Decisions about personal belongings aren't usually made during ideal circumstances. Frequently these decisions are made during stressful times, such as when a death has occurred or when an elderly family member is moving to a health care facility or apartment. Decision making becomes more challenging and sensitive when family members are in the process of grieving the loss of a family member, selling the home they grew up in, or facing the increasing dependence of an elder. While not easy, decisions about the transfer of personal property can be a time to reminisce, share memories, and work through the grieving process.

Different Perceptions of What's Fair

When the value of property can't be easily measured in dollars, the challenge of transferring property becomes more sensitive. Different ideas about what is fair can make the process and the results of property transfer decisions frustrating, hurtful, and damaging to relationships. On the other hand, taking time to understand the different perceptions of what's fair can reduce misunderstandings, help family members learn about each other's wishes, and strengthen relationships among family members.

Reality of Family Experiences

Attorneys who work with estate planning say that often the personal property, not the titled property, causes the most problems when settling an estate. Material possessions seem to become more valuable and have a greater potential for conflict when titled property or the rest of the estate is small.

Adult siblings have been known to break off relationships with each other over how personal property was divided. Unresolved family issues and feelings of unfairness can continue to influence the transfer of personal property. Many people have stories about successful or unsuccessful transfers of personal belongings in their family. These continue to be remembered and shared.

Adult siblings have been known to break off relationships with each other over how personal property was divided.

Beginning the Process

For some, beginning a conversation about a sensitive issue is the most difficult part of communicating. Here are two ways to open a conversation about transferring personal property.

1. Ask "what if" questions.

For example, "Dad, what would you want to have happen with the things in the house if you and Mom were no longer able to live here? What concerns or special wishes would you have? What if we had to make decisions about what happens to some of your belongings, like your gun collection or family photographs?"

Or you might say, "Aunt Ellen, what would happen if you were in a car accident and were unable to handle your affairs? You have a house full of memories and fourteen nieces and nephews. Have you decided who would be responsible for distributing your things? How would you want this handled?"

Asking any of these "what if"s can create anxiety for both the person raising the questions and the person trying to answer. You may reassure the owner by saying, "Chances are you will be living here for a long time, but if this would be needed, I'd like to know your wishes."

Using "I" Statements to Communicate

When you have strong feelings, it is important to express yourself so others don't take offense. The way you state your thoughts and feelings should be non-threatening and non-blaming. This is often done with "I" messages, or personal expressions of feelings, concerns, and needs.

Here is a sample "I" statement:

"Dad, since Mom has been ill and we started talking about moving you to an apartment in town, I've been worried about how decisions will be made about sorting through all your things. I've tried to bring this up before, and I'm concerned that if we don't talk about this soon, Mom won't be able to participate in making the decisions."

(For more suggestions on effective communications, see "Chapter 8: Managing Conflicts if they Arise.")

2. Look for natural opportunities to talk.

When a friend or relative is dealing with transferring personal belongings, use the situation to introduce a discussion. Or, describe the situation of a friend or relative who recently experienced dividing up property. Follow up the story by asking, "What would you have done if you were in that situation?"

Don't assume you are the only one in your family that is concerned about this issue. A similar approach may be used to initiate conversations with siblings, children, co-owners of property, or others who may share your desire to open a dialogue.

If others refuse to talk, or deny the possibility of ever having to deal with the situation, you cannot force their involvement. You do have the right to share your feelings. Don't be afraid to raise the issue. You may feel better because you made an effort.

Avoiding the Issue

Sensitive issues, such as the transfer of personal belongings, are difficult not only to bring up but also to talk about in any depth. It is hard to approach an issue calmly when there are strong feelings about what is important, what needs to happen, and how things should be done. Sometimes individuals may not see personal property as an issue to be addressed. They may refuse to talk about it. There may be differences of opinion and conflicting views among family members.

Have you used any of the following reasons to avoid the issue of transferring personal property? This review of the arguments for tackling sensitive issues might be helpful.

Avoiding the Issue

Reasons Used to Avoid Issues	Remember...
Bringing up death is disrespectful and uncomfortable.	Few individuals want to give the impression that family members might die or that we want someone to die. While death is a difficult part of the life cycle for most people to accept and talk about, it will happen to each of us. Many people say they feel relieved and in control when such discussions take place and decisions are made.
It won't be a problem in my family.	Most people like to believe their family will be the exception and are surprised when there are different perceptions of what's fair when conflicts arise. If no problems are expected, communicating and planning should go smoothly.
I don't have anything of value.	Assumptions are too often made about the emotional value others might place on your personal property. Just because no one has asked about your property does not indicate a lack of interest. When they ask, most people are surprised to learn what has meaning to others.
Others might think I'm greedy.	Tell others your needs and intentions using "I" statements. Let others know why you think decisions should be made now. Getting the decision-making process started does not mean you will always get your way. Talk about how decisions will be made and carried out.

Avoiding the Issue (cont.)

Reasons Used to Avoid Issues	Remember...
It may not be my place or role.	Even if you are an in-law, you are a member of the family—and since you came to the family as an adult, you may be in a better position to initiate the subject than other family members. In-laws are affected by decisions about personal property.
No one will listen anyway.	Not speaking up means that others will not know your opinions and feelings. Tell them your needs using "I" statements. Others may have similar concerns and fears.
I'm too young to worry about death.	While death is hard for most to accept, it doesn't keep it from happening. Just as there are decisions that must go with living, there are decisions related to dying. If you choose not to make those decisions, others will be forced to make them for you. Family members, a personal representative, or the courts may have to deal with frustration and lack of agreement because no one knew your intentions or goals.
Things will never be the same.	Decisions about personal belongings often come at times of loss or transition. Such transitions may bring closure to a time past, but not to the memories attached to that time and place. Objects, and the memories associated with them, help keep memories alive and provide continuity. Recognize the importance of the grieving process—whether for persons or places.

Avoiding the Issue (cont.)

Reasons Used to Avoid Issues	Remember...
There are too many other issues to cope with.	There is never an ideal time to deal with property transfer issues. Such decisions are part of larger and more complex issues related to transitions and death—none of which will disappear.
Family members will never agree.	Different perceptions and expectations are normal, especially in regard to what's fair. Taking time to understand different viewpoints can help avoid misunderstandings and may lead to respectfully agreeing to disagree.
We don't talk about feelings in my family.	Talking about sentimental value and feelings may be uncomfortable for some family members. Making assumptions can lead to conflicts and misunderstandings, which may lead to even greater problems.
Past conflicts and feelings between family members will create problems.	Conflicts from past family history can emerge and influence decisions about property transfer. Avoiding the issue won't make your family history go away. Talking with each other and working out potential conflicts before a family crisis can help improve decision making. Focus on the issue at hand instead of unrelated conflicts. Encourage the use of "I" statements to understand the needs and goals of all involved.

"It's not just the objects themselves but the meanings and feelings that sustain one's life that are at issue. Family members need to be sensitive to and have respect for the feelings and meanings involved."

— Csikszentmihalyi and Rochberg-Halton, 1981

Tips on Talking About Sensitive Issues

The following are some tips to keep in mind when you are planning to talk about sensitive topics, such as transferring personal property. (See also "Chapter 8: Managing Conflicts if they Arise.")

- Know the issue you want to bring up. Outline the major points in writing. What role do you want the other person to play? For example, do you want them to listen, to act, to express ideas, or to just be there?

- Know why you want to talk about transferring personal property. What are your concerns? What prompted the concern now? What is to be gained by discussing this? What problems could arise by discussing this?

- Rehearse or practice what you might say—even if it is just to yourself in the bathroom or car. You may have a close friend who can play the role of the other person to make it more realistic.

- Choose a time and make an appointment with the other person, making sure that telephone, television, radio, or visitors will not distract you. If the time agreed upon for the discussion is changed because of circumstances, make another appointment.

- Use "I" statements to describe how you feel, what the issue is, and what you hope might happen as a result of the discussion. Avoid messages that focus on what you want the other person to do, say, or feel.

- Use the *Who Gets Grandma's Yellow Pie Plate?™ Video*, if available, to introduce others to the subject of transferring non-titled property. (See page ii for order information.)

- Stay focused on the topic of transferring personal property. Avoid bringing up other issues. If the other person brings up unrelated topics, gently (but firmly) return to the topic at hand.

- Be prepared to respond to questions. Attempt to listen to the other person's concerns, his or her interpretation of what you said, and his or her reaction. Be able to clarify your intention if it is misinterpreted. Provide clear feedback.

- Ask questions to clarify what you have heard.

- Finish the conversation when the issue you wanted discussed has been clarified, even though there may not be any resolution at this time. The more sensitive the issue, the more likely the need for some "thinking time" alone. If necessary, be prepared to resume the discussion later, at a time agreeable to all.

Allow "thinking time" for people to process issues.

▶ Next Step

Now that you've opened the discussion with your spouse, family members or others, the next step is to determine what you want to accomplish. "Chapter 3: Determine What You Want to Accomplish" will help you and others sort out your goals.

Notes:

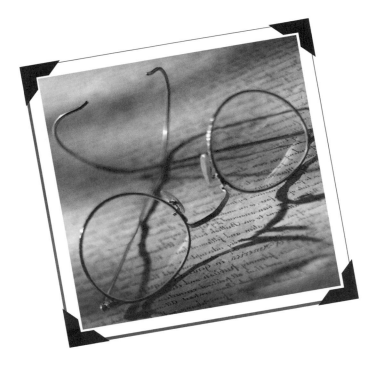

Chapter 3:   Determine What You Want to Accomplish

by Marlene S. Stum, University of Minnesota Extension and Department of Family Social Science

As a young boy my mother started me out with a stamp collection. I've been collecting stamps for over fifty years now.

My wife and I have been making a list of who should get what things when we die. She says I need to decide about my stamp collection. I've talked to each of our three children and none of them seem interested. Our grandchildren, nieces and nephews aren't interested either.

I know I could sell it for at least $10,000 but I don't want to. I would really like someone in my family to care about it, to carry on the tradition, and to get as much pleasure out of the collection as I have.

— Raksha

Sorting Out Goals

What is it that you hope to accomplish when your non-titled property is transferred? Have you thought about what's most important to you? If you have a co-owner, such as a spouse, do you know what's most important to them? Have you really taken time to think about, share, and discuss your transfer goals? Do people who will receive your personal property know what you are hoping to accomplish?

An important part of transferring personal property is identifying your goals, and coming to an agreement on what you want to accomplish with any co-owners. Many people feel tempted to skip this part of the transfer process. Why do goals need to be identified? Identifying your goals will help you determine what you and other co-owners want to happen. Not everyone has the same goals. Once goals are identified it is easier to decide how to best accomplish them. For example, if one of your goals in transferring possessions is to maintain privacy, you can select property distribution methods that keep decisions among family members. Another benefit of identifying goals is being able to let potential receivers know what you are trying to accomplish. This can help avoid misunderstandings and assumptions about your intentions.

The following goals are frequently identified as important when transferring non-titled property:

- Maintaining privacy;
- Improving family relationships;
- Being fair to all involved;
- Preserving memories; and
- Contributing to society.

Worksheet 2 will help you identify goals that are priorities for you. There may be other goals you want to accomplish that need to be added. In many cases, not all goals can be accomplished at the same time and decisions must be made about which goals are more important than others.

Worksheet 2 Potential Transfer Goals

Name: _____ Date: _____

Directions: Read each goal and identify how important it is to you by placing a mark on the line indicating that it is "not at all important," somewhere in the middle, or "very important." If the goal does not seem to apply to you or your situation, simply leave it blank. There is room to add goals important to you that aren't already listed. Answer the questions at the end of the worksheet to summarize your transfer goals. It is best to identify goals on your own before sharing with others in the family.

Importance of Maintaining Privacy

Not at all important — Very important

1. Decisions about my personal property should be kept in the family

2. Public auctions or sales for distribution of personal property should be avoided

3. Court involvement in personal property distribution should be avoided

Importance of Family Relationships

Not at all important — Very important

1. Everyone in my family is still talking to each other after belongings are transferred

2. Feelings of resentment or anger are minimized among members of my family

3. Family members agree to work out disagreements and conflicts

4. Family members cooperate as decisions are made

5. Family members agree with what I want to do with family belongings

6. Family members can be honest and open about items received or to be received

Worksheet 2: Potential Transfer Goals (cont.)

Importance of Being Fair to All Involved

Not at all important — Very important

1. My personal property is transferred so that everyone is treated equally or the same, regardless of any differences (needs, contributions, status of family member, etc.)

2. Differences among family members are taken into account when personal property is transferred so that family members are treated equitably

3. All concerned family members have a chance for their point of view to be heard as decisions are made

4. Decisions about "who gets what" are consistently applied to all involved

5. The process of how decisions are made about transfers is consistent for all persons and over time

Importance of Preserving Memories

Not at all important — Very important

1. Belongings go to individuals in my family who will truly value and appreciate them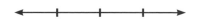

2. Belongings go to individuals who are most likely to pass on items in the same spirit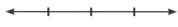

3. Belongings go to people who will remember my family history and heritage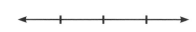

4. Belongings are passed on to future generations who have a connection to me

Worksheet 2: Potential Transfer Goals (cont.)

Importance of Contributing to Society

Not at all important — Very important

1 Selected belongings are given to benefit the public (museums, historical society, etc.)

2 Collections are donated to benefit the public (i.e., museums)

3 Selected belongings are sold with proceeds given to a chosen cause

Other Goals

Are there goals other than those mentioned that you would like to accomplish when transferring your non-titled property? List them below.

Not at all important — Very important

1

2

3

Worksheet 2: Potential Transfer Goals (cont.)

 # What Did You Learn?

Go back and review how you rated each category.

Which category of goals (for example, preserving memories, being fair, or one listed above) is most important? List one or more below.

1

2

Which category is least important? List one or more below.

1

2

This worksheet was written by Marlene S. Stum, University of Minnesota Extension and Department of Family Social Science.

In accordance with the Americans with Disabilities Act, this worksheet is available in alternative formats upon request. Direct requests to 1-800-876-8636.

University of Minnesota Extension is an equal opportunity educator and employer.

Visit us online at www.yellowpieplate.umn.edu.

▶ Next Steps

- If there are co-owners of the non-titled property, ask them to complete "Worksheet 2: Potential Transfer Goals" on their own and then compare answers. Where do you agree or disagree about what you hope to accomplish? Differences in goals are normal. Strategies for improving communication and resolving conflicts may be helpful. (See "Chapter 8: Managing Conflicts if they Arise.")

- Let your list of goals—both most and least important—help guide your decisions through the rest of the personal property transfer process. For example, if you have rated several lines under "Importance of Family Relationships" as "very important," then this is a goal you value highly, so negotiating and communicating are probably very important to you. If you have answered under "Maintaining Privacy" that it is "not at all important" in several cases, then that may have little influence on your decisions. This might mean, for example, that you could use public sales to dispose of property.

- If you ranked being fair to all as an important goal, it is especially important that you move on to "Chapter 4: "Determine What Fair Means." Additional worksheets found in that chapter can help both owners and potential receivers of property clarify what they think is fair.

- Communicate what you hope to accomplish to those who will receive your personal property as well as to those who may be responsible for carrying out your wishes (such as a personal representative). Doing this will help others understand your intentions and reduce misunderstandings.

Notes:

Chapter 4: Determine What Fair Means

by Marlene S. Stum, University of Minnesota Extension and Department of Family Social Science

When Mom died, my sisters and I had already graduated from high school and left home. Several years later, Dad remarried and his new wife moved into 'our home.'

When Dad died, many of the items that belonged to my parents stayed in the house with my stepmother. Once she died, all of our parent's belongings—and the memories that went with them—went to my stepmother's children.

We still feel hurt and angry when we see the milk glass candy dish from our family at our stepsister's house. The dish was given to my parents as a wedding gift. It's just not fair! Why should she have it?

— Laysha

Being Fair is Important to Many

Many people will say they want to be fair to all the members of their family when their belongings are transferred. What does "fair" mean? There can be many different ideas of what makes both the process and outcome fair. What assumptions do members of your family have about what is fair when transferring non-titled personal property?

In some families it is considered fair when selected personal items are passed on to the oldest. In other families it is considered a fair process to allow only siblings to choose or receive items— no in-laws are allowed. What unwritten rules or assumptions have been used in your family to pass on non-titled personal property? Are there examples of times when the process of transfer, or who got what, was considered unfair?

Does Fair Always Mean Equal?

Fair does not always mean equal. Some family members consider the distribution of belongings to be fair when everyone has received an equal amount. In this case, differences among family members are not emphasized. When dealing with non-titled property, challenges quickly arise about whether "equal" means an equal number of items, equal dollar value, or equal in terms of emotional

Different perceptions about what is fair are inevitable. Fair is not always equal.

value. What makes dividing equally even more difficult is that the sentimental meaning or value of items will differ for each individual. What one person considers of equal emotional value may not at all be what another would consider equal. Some personal belongings may or may not have a great deal of financial value.

Who determines the value of an item? Is value measured in emotional terms, dollars and cents, or some combination? Some individuals prefer to take differences among family members into account with a desire to be equitable when transferring personal belongings. Things taken into account can include contributions over the years (like care or gifts), needs (i.e., financial, emotional, or physical), and other differences among family members such as age, birth order, or marital status.

Consider a Fair Process

Some people feel that using a fair process is more important than who actually gets what items. For example, family members may feel good about the end result if each person's viewpoint is heard and if the lottery system used to divide up important items is agreed upon by all involved. Different feelings about who should be involved and when transfers should occur can be the source of many disagreements. The issue of who is and isn't "family" can quickly arise. Is it fair if one daughter-in-law is involved and the sons-in-law are not? Is it fair that one son gets to receive items now, while other siblings have to wait?

Understand What "Fair" Means in Your Family

Different perceptions about what is fair are inevitable and normal. It can be extremely helpful to identify the unwritten rules or assumptions behind what is considered fair to members of your family.

Recognize that there are no right answers. Property owners have the legal right to decide when and how to transfer their non-titled property. However, understanding different perceptions about what is fair can help avoid making assumptions that are not necessarily true. It can be helpful for owners to let others know what rules they are using to decide who gets what and to communicate clearly what process is being used to make decisions. While there are many points of view, communicating can help reduce inaccurate assumptions, misunderstandings, and unnecessary tensions. Family members may also respectfully agree to disagree.

It can also be helpful when talking about fairness to agree to resolve conflicts, if they arise. Suggestions are offered in "Chapter 8: Managing Conflicts if they Arise."

The next two worksheets help both owners and potential receivers of non-titled property determine what fair means.

- Property owners should fill out Worksheet 3, parts A and B.
- Potential property receivers should fill out Worksheet 4, parts A and B.

Each family member who is involved in decision making should answer the appropriate worksheet separately. Answers can then be compared to understand how beliefs are similar and different.

Worksheet 3 Owners of Non-titled Property Determine What Fair Means

Name: _____ Date: _____

Directions: This worksheet can help you as a property owner become more aware of your assumptions and beliefs about what would be "fair" in both the process and end result of who gets what belongings. Read each statement and identify how important it is to you by placing a mark on the line indicating that it is "not at all important," somewhere in the middle, or "very important." If the statement does not apply to you or your family situation, simply leave it blank. Part A will help you determine rules for deciding. If needed, add your own rules about what would make something fair as you go along. Part B will help you decide how to decide. Answer the questions at the end of each section to summarize your perceptions of what fair means. It is best to complete both parts of this worksheet on your own before sharing it with others.

Part A: Owners Determine Rules for Deciding

Importance of Treating Everyone Equally

		Not at all important	Very important
1	Family members are treated the same regardless of what they may have contributed to the family over the years		
2	Family members are treated the same regardless of differences in needs		
3	Family members are treated the same regardless of differences (such as birth order, gender, or marital status)		
4	Family members receive equal numbers of items, regardless of sentimental meaning		
5	Family members receive equal numbers of items which have sentimental meaning to them		
6	Family members receive equal dollar value of appraised items		
7	Family members all have an equal chance of getting items that more than one might want regardless of financial resources (drawing names, lottery system, taking turns at selecting, using chips or pretend money, etc.)		

Worksheet 3: Owners of Non-titled Property Determine What Fair Means
Part A: Owners Determine Rules for Deciding (cont.)

Importance of Recognizing Different Contributions

	Not at all important	Very important

1 | Items received as gifts from family members be given back to the same giver

2 | Family members who have helped do work around the home or business be rewarded

3 | Family members who have helped me financially are rewarded

4 | Family members who have helped provide care and support over the years are rewarded

5 | Family members who have shown me the most love are rewarded

6 | Organizations or individuals outside of family are rewarded

Importance of Recognizing Different Needs

	Not at all important	Very important

1 | Family members with financial needs receive more

2 | Family members with physical or disability needs receive more

3 | Family members with greater emotional needs receive more

Worksheet 3: Owners of Non-titled Property Determine What Fair Means
Part A: Owners Determine Rules for Deciding (cont.)

Importance of Recognizing Differences Among Family Members

		Not at all important	Very important
1	Birth order (i.e. oldest or youngest) influences who receives specific items		
2	Current age influences who receives specific items		
3	Whether someone is male or female influences what they receive		
4	Whether family members are married, widowed, divorced, or never married influences what they receive		
5	Whether family members have children by birth, adoption, or remarriage influences what they receive		
6	Whether family members live close or at a distance influences what they receive		
7	Whether family members have a personal interest in the item influences what they receive		

Worksheet 3: Owners of Non-titled Property Determine What Fair Means
Part A: Owners Determine Rules for Deciding (cont.)

What Did You Learn About Deciding Who Gets What?

Go back and review your ratings in each category. For each of the following questions, pick the answer that best summarizes your ratings.

- Is it more important to you to:

    _____ Treat everyone equally so that all get the same
    _____ Take into account differences among family members

- If treating people equally is important, what does "equal" mean to you?

    _____ Equal financial value
    _____ Equal in emotional value
    _____ Equal numbers of items regardless of emotional value
    _____ Equal numbers of items that are meaningful

- If differences are taken into account, which types of differences are more important to you?

    _____ Differences in contributions
    _____ Differences in needs
    _____ Differences among family members such as birth order, marital status, or personal interests
    _____ Other:

What rules did you rate most important? List them below.

What rules did you rate least important? List them below.

Worksheet 3: Owners of Non-titled Property Determine What Fair Means
Part B: Owners Decide How to Decide

Importance of When Decisions Are Made

Not at all important — Very important

1 Determining who gets what now, while I am able to make decisions

2 Giving selected items away before my death to whom I choose

3 Putting my wishes in writing and mentioning in my will

4 Letting my personal representative decide what happens to my belongings after I die

5 Letting surviving family members decide what happens to my belongings after I die

6 Preventing family members from taking items without my knowing

7 Responding to requests for items from family members

Importance of Who Is Involved In Decisions

Not at all important — Very important

1 Asking my children what they would like to receive

2 Asking the spouses of my children what they would like to receive

3 Asking my grandchildren what they would like to receive

4 Having items of financial value appraised by someone outside the family

5 Informing family members what decisions I have made as the owner

6 Making decisions when all can be present

Worksheet 3: Owners of Non-titled Property Determine What Fair Means
Part B: Owners Decide How to Decide (cont.)

What Did You Learn About
A Fair Transfer Process?

Go back and review how important you said each of the statements was in each category.

When should transfer decisions be made and carried out? List the information below.

Who do you believe should be involved in the process? List them below.

Worksheet 3: Owners of Non-titled Property Determine What Fair Means (cont.)

> ### ▶ Next Steps: Owners of Non-titled Property
>
> - Compare your responses on this worksheet with those of your children or other possible receivers who have completed similar questions designed for potential receivers of your non-titled property (Worksheet 4, Parts A and B). Decisions legally rest with the property owners while alive; however, discussing and understanding different ideas about what is fair can help avoid making assumptions that are not true.
>
> - Compare your perceptions of what is fair with co-owners of the non-titled property. Are there differences in what would be considered fair? Are there differences about who should get what or about the process of deciding? On what points do you agree? On what points can you reach a compromise? Are there points on which you can agree to disagree?
>
> - Remember that different perceptions about what is fair are normal. There are no right answers.
>
> - Continue on to "Chapter 5: Identify Special Objects to Transfer."

This worksheet was written by Marlene S. Stum, University of Minnesota Extension and Department of Family Social Science.

In accordance with the Americans with Disabilities Act, this worksheet is available in alternative formats upon request. Direct requests to 1-800-876-8636.

University of Minnesota Extension is an equal opportunity educator and employer.

Visit us online at www.yellowpieplate.umn.edu.

Worksheet 4 **Potential Receivers of Non-titled Property Determine What Fair Means**

Name: _____ Date: _____

Directions: This worksheet can help you, as a potential receiver of another person's non-titled property, become more aware of your assumptions and beliefs about what would be "fair" in both the process and end result of who gets what belongings. Read each statement and identify how important it is to you by placing a mark on the line indicating that it is "not at all important," somewhere in the middle, or "very important." If the statement does not apply to you or your family situation, simply leave it blank. Part A will help you determine rules for deciding. If needed, add your own rules about what would make something fair as you go along. Part B will help you decide how to decide. Answer the questions at the end of each section to summarize your perceptions of what fair means. It is best to complete both parts of this worksheet on your own before sharing it with others.

Part A: Receivers Determine Rules for Deciding

Importance of Treating Everyone Equally

		Not at all important	Very important

1 Family members are treated the same regardless of what they may have contributed to the family over the years

2 Family members are treated the same regardless of differences in needs

3 Family members are treated the same regardless of differences (such as birth order, gender, or marital status)

4 Family members receive equal numbers of items, regardless of sentimental meaning

5 Family members receive equal numbers of items which have sentimental meaning to them

6 Family members receive equal dollar value of appraised items

7 Family members all have an equal chance of getting items that more than one might want regardless of financial resources (drawing names, lottery system, taking turns at selecting, using chips or pretend money, etc.)

Worksheet 4: Potential Receivers of Non-titled Property Determine What Fair Means
Part A: Receivers Determine Rules for Deciding (cont.)

Importance of Recognizing Different Contributions

		Not at all important	Very important
1	Items received as gifts from family members be given back to the same giver		◄—┼—┼—┼—►
2	Family members who have helped do work around the home or business be rewarded		◄—┼—┼—┼—►
3	Family members who helped financially are rewarded		◄—┼—┼—┼—►
4	Family members who helped provide care and support over the years are rewarded		◄—┼—┼—┼—►
5	Family members who have shown the most love are rewarded		◄—┼—┼—┼—►
6	Organizations or individuals outside of family are rewarded		◄—┼—┼—┼—►

Importance of Recognizing Different Needs

		Not at all important	Very important
1	Family members with financial needs receive more		◄—┼—┼—┼—►
2	Family members with physical or disability needs receive more		◄—┼—┼—┼—►
3	Family members with greater emotional needs receive more		◄—┼—┼—┼—►

Worksheet 4: Potential Receivers of Non-titled Property Determine What Fair Means
Part A: Receivers Determine Rules for Deciding (cont.)

Importance of Recognizing Differences Among Family Members

		Not at all important			Very important
1	Birth order (i.e. oldest or youngest) influences who receives specific items				
2	Current age influences who receives specific items				
3	Whether someone is male or female influences what they receive				
4	Whether family members are married, widowed, divorced, or never married influences what they receive				
5	Whether family members have children by birth, adoption, or remarriage influences what they receive				
6	Whether family members live close or at a distance influences what they receive				
7	Whether family members have a personal interest in the item influences what they receive				

What Did You Learn About Deciding Who Gets What?

Go back and review your ratings in each category. For each of the following questions, pick the answer that best summarizes your ratings.

- Is it more important to you to:

  _____ Treat everyone equally so that all get the same
  _____ Take into account differences among family members

- If treating people equally is important, what does "equal" mean to you?

  _____ Equal financial value
  _____ Equal in emotional value
  _____ Equal numbers of items regardless of emotional value
  _____ Equal numbers of items that are meaningful

- If differences are taken into account, which types of differences are more important to you?

  _____ Differences in contributions
  _____ Differences in needs
  _____ Differences among family members such as birth order, marital status, or personal interests
  _____ Other (list):

What rules did you rate most important? List them below.

What rules did you rate least important? List them below.

Worksheet 4: Potential Receivers of Non-titled Property Determine What Fair Means (cont.)

Part B: Receivers Determine How to Decide

Importance of When Decisions Are Made

Not at all important   Very important

1 Owners determine who gets what now while they are able to make decisions

2 Owners give selected items away before they die

3 Owners put wishes in writing and mention in their wills

4 Personal representative decides what happens to belongings at death

5 Surviving family members decide what happens to belongings at death

6 Family members are prevented from taking items without others knowing

7 Owners respond to requests for items from family members

Importance of Who Is Involved in Decisions

Not at all important   Very important

1 Children asked what they would like to receive

2 Spouses of children asked what they would like to receive

3 Grandchildren asked what they would like to receive

4 Having items of financial value appraised by someone outside the family

5 Family members informed what decisions owners have made

6 Making decisions when all can be present

Worksheet 4: Potential Receivers of Non-titled Property Determine What Fair Means

Part B: Receivers Determine How to Decide (cont.)

 # What Did You Learn About A Fair Transfer Process?

Go back and review how important you said each of the statements was in each category.

When should transfer decisions be made and carried out? List the information below.

Who do you believe should be involved in the process? List the information below.

Worksheet 4: Potential Receivers of Non-titled Property Determine What Fair Means (cont.)

> ### ▶ Next Steps: Potential Receivers of Non-titled Property
>
> - Compare your responses on this worksheet with siblings or others who might also have a stake in how personal belongings are transferred. Are there differences in what each considers fair? Are there differences about who should get what or about the process of deciding? On what points do you agree? Are there points on which you can compromise?
>
> - Compare your perceptions of what is fair with those of your parents or the owners of the non-titled property who have completed similar questions (Worksheet 3, Part A and B). Decisions legally rest with the property owners while alive; however, discussing and understanding different viewpoints can help avoid making assumptions that are not true. When someone dies, personal belongings become part of their estate. A personal representative, such as an executor, is empowered to make and carry out decisions.
>
> - Remember, different perceptions about what is fair are normal. There are no right answers.
>
> - Continue on to "Chapter 5: Identify Special Objects to Transfer."

This worksheet was written by Marlene S. Stum, University of Minnesota Extension and Department of Family Social Science.

In accordance with the Americans with Disabilities Act, this worksheet is available in alternative formats upon request. Direct requests to 1-800-876-8636.

University of Minnesota Extension is an equal opportunity educator and employer.

Visit us online at www.yellowpieplate.umn.edu.

I was very surprised when three of my seven adult children said they wanted a 25¢ Christmas tree ornament that had special memories for each of them. It is a carousel-shaped ornament with a red metal fan inside that spins around when placed over the heat of a tree bulb. As the children were growing up, they were fascinated with it.

I still have the challenge of deciding which one of the three should receive the decoration. However, without asking, I would never have known that it was special to them.

— Norma

Chapter 5:   Identify Special Objects to Transfer

by Marlene S. Stum, University of Minnesota Extension Service, Department of Family Social Science

One evening last week I stopped by my parents' house to visit. Mom had gone to a gathering that afternoon where they were asked to bring the oldest item they had in their home. Mom said, 'I took the silver pen your dad got from Father Greiner when he served Mass as a child. Father Greiner brought it over from the Netherlands when he immigrated.'

Later that evening it struck me that at 43 years old, I had never seen this pen or heard the story before. Had we been cleaning out my parents possessions after death, I wouldn't have known a thing about the pen or its history.

— David

Meanings Will Differ

What are the "pie plates" in your life? They may not be round and they may not be yellow, but look around your home for the special personal belongings in your family. Answers will vary when different family members identify special items and explain their importance. Do you know which of your belongings might be special to others and why?

While Grandma's yellow pie plate might be important to you, it may not be important to others in your family. Make no assumptions about what someone else might value or why. The value given belongings by someone who is 83 years old may be different from that of someone who is 57 or 23 years old. Grandpa's journal may seem like just a dust collector to a grandchild who is currently 17, but may be considered a treasure full of family history when that grandchild is 47 years of age, or vice versa. A husband and wife may name the same special objects, but give different reasons why the item is special to them. When naming special objects, mothers and daughters tend to be more alike in their answers than fathers and sons.

Potential List of Cherished Objects
Furniture
Plates/dishes/utensils
Handmade items (quilts, stitchery, tables and chairs, etc.)
Electronic equipment (i.e. TV or CDs)
Antiques
Linens and needlework
Musical instruments
Jewelry
Guns
Tools
Pets
Art pieces (i.e. pictures or vases)
Collections (coins, plates, stamps, etc.)
Photographs
Written material (Bibles, book of poems written by Grandma, diaries, letters, etc.)
Documents or records (marriage certificates, awards, military discharge papers, etc.)

Identify Special Items

An important step in making decisions about transferring non-titled property is to make a list of special objects. Then share the meaning attached to each item. Tell what makes it special and share your feelings about who should receive the item and why. Worksheet 5 can help owners ask and answer these important questions.

Pets require special consideration in this process. Decisions about pets can be emotionally charged and provoke conflict within families, yet it is not uncommon for those decisions to be overlooked. Also, the person receiving the pet will inherit a significant responsibility along with the animal. It is important to be sure that the person identified as the recipient of the pet knows, understands and is prepared to accept this responsibility.

Gather Input from Others

Many parents choose to gather information from their children, grandchildren, or others before deciding what to pass on to others. Worksheet 6 can be used by children, grandchildren, other family members or friends to help gather information from potential receivers of your personal possessions. Don't be surprised to find differences and similarities in the lists.

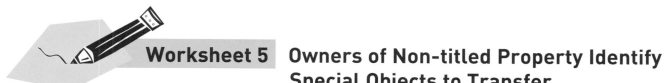

Name: _____ Date: _____

Directions: What special non-titled property do you have which you hope to pass on or transfer to others? Describe the items below.

Describe Item:	Why is this Item Special?	Who Should Receive It? Why?

This worksheet was written by Marlene S. Stum, University of Minnesota Extension and Department of Family Social Science.

In accordance with the Americans with Disabilities Act, this worksheet is available in alternative formats upon request. Direct requests to 1-800-876-8636.

University of Minnesota Extension is an equal opportunity educator and employer.

Visit us online at www.yellowpieplate.umn.edu.

Worksheet 6 Potential Receivers Identify Special Objects to Transfer

Name: _____ Date: _____

Part A: Your Hopes for Yourself

Directions: What special personal belongings or non-titled property do your parents have which you hope they will pass on or transfer to you? Describe those items using the following table.

Describe Item:	This Item is Special to Me Because…	If Someone Else Received this Item I Would Feel…

Worksheet 6: Potential Receivers Identify Special Objects to Transfer (cont.)
Part B: Your Wishes for Others

Directions: Are there special objects/possessions your parent(s) have which you hope they will pass on or transfer to people other than yourself? Describe those items using the following table.

Describe Item:	This Item Should Go to...	Because...

This worksheet was written by Marlene S. Stum, University of Minnesota Extension and Department of Family Social Science.

In accordance with the Americans with Disabilities Act, this worksheet is available in alternative formats upon request. Direct requests to 1-800-876-8636.

University of Minnesota Extension is an equal opportunity educator and employer.

Visit us online at www.yellowpieplate.umn.edu.

Sharing stories and meanings about significant belongings helps preserve family history, memories and traditions.

Tell the Stories

Special family belongings serve as props to tell family stories. No matter what your ethnic origin, and no matter how recently family members may have arrived in the United States, do not assume that objects used every day have more (or less) importance than belongings of previous generations.

Objects add meaning to celebrations and events. It is impossible to remember events without recalling the objects involved with those events. Holiday dinner memories include the feel of the linen tablecloth, images of the china pattern and silverware, the butter dish with the missing cover, the wallpaper with smudges around the light-switch plate, and the glowing candles.

Telling stories about special objects helps family members understand their past, discover another side of their family, and appreciate the accomplishments of their ancestors. Without consciously asking about family history, a person may have a dim and distorted vision of the past. Worksheet 7 can help you share stories and meanings about significant belongings. Sharing answers to the questions on the worksheet can help tell the stories and preserve family history, memories, and traditions. The process of sharing may be accomplished by talking, by writing the information, by recording in audio or video, or by any combination of these methods.

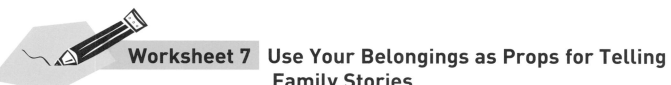

Worksheet 7 Use Your Belongings as Props for Telling Family Stories

Name: _____ Date: _____

Directions: Do you have special memories about a particular belonging? Capture that memory by answering the following questions about the item. Make a copy of this worksheet for each item you want to describe.

Name of item:

When did you acquire it?

How did you acquire it?

When and how have you used it?

Who else owned it before you?

Worksheet 7: Use Your Belongings as Props for Telling Family Stories (cont.)

Who do you want to give it to when you no longer need it?

Why do you want this person to receive it?

What other memories do you have of this item?

What memories do you have of the people who owned this before you?

This worksheet was written by Marlene S. Stum, University of Minnesota Extension and Department of Family Social Science.

In accordance with the Americans with Disabilities Act, this worksheet is available in alternative formats upon request. Direct requests to 1-800-876-8636.

University of Minnesota Extension is an equal opportunity educator and employer.

Visit us online at www.yellowpieplate.umn.edu.

▶ Next Step

Once there is a working list of the objects that need to be transferred, there are numerous methods for distributing them. "Chapter 6: Distribution Options and Consequences," will help you explore a variety of distribution options and consequences of each.

Notes:

Chapter 6:   Distribution Options and Consequences

by Claire Althoff and Christy Bubolz, University of Minnesota Extension Service

When my grandfather died in late spring, he left a list of what items should go to whom in the family.

Rather than disposing of these items immediately after the funeral, our family chose to reconvene at Thanksgiving for what we called 'The Great Giveaway.' After a wonderful turkey dinner, Grandpa's list was read and each person received the items designated for him or her. As they did so, each took time to share their memories of the fun times and special moments they had shared with Grandpa.

I will always remember it as a very special day.

— Sandy

Families use a variety of methods to distribute non-titled property. No method is "perfect" or "right" for all families. In order for families to find the best method for their situation, they need to first identify goals and then keep these goals in mind as they select the distribution method they will use. (See "Chapter 3: Determining What You Want to Accomplish.")

It is important for the individuals involved to discuss, identify, and agree upon a method, or methods, of transfer before beginning the distribution process. Whether the goal of distribution is maintaining privacy, preserving memories, having good family relationships, contributing to society or being fair to everyone involved, the method(s) used should help participants achieve the property distribution goals which have been identified. While families should be creative as they seek solutions to any problems that arise, they also need to be aware of laws governing the transfer of non-titled property in their state, and work within the legal guidelines.

The time at which decisions are made will influence potential methods of distribution. Decisions about the transfer of non-titled property may be made:

1. Prior to death or other crisis by the property owner, or

2. After death by the relatives, friends, and/or personal representative of the owner.

When Emma invited her four children to spend a day with her and requested that no grandchildren or spouses come, her children wondered what was up. At the time, their 85-year-old mother was planning to move from her home of 45 years to a nursing home.

The children gathered and spent the day going through Emma's property with her. Emma took an item, talked about where it came from and then the family talked about their memories related to the item. Next they decided who should have each item.

Nine months later when Emma died, the children couldn't help but appreciate the special day they had shared together with their mother before she died. What a wonderful celebration of her life it had been!

— Cindy

When property owners make decisions prior to death, it allows the person transferring the property to consider the wishes of the recipients and pay attention to special memories shared with the recipients. Doing so may help to eliminate misunderstandings about the owner's wishes. When decisions are made after a death, they may not accurately reflect the wishes of the owner. Very often more than one person feels they have been promised, or are entitled to, the same item.

Distribution methods that require planning prior to death include gifting, labeling items, making a will, and preparing lists of property specifying the intended recipient. Auctions and other types of sales held either within the family or for the general public, or an in-family distribution utilizing some kind of selection, such as a lottery, may occur either before or after the death of the property owner. These methods are frequently used when a person moves into smaller living quarters (for example, moving from a house to an apartment or long-term care facility), as well as after the owner's death. When owners fail to plan for non-titled property transfer prior to their death, distribution options become more limited.

Regardless of when the transfer decisions are made and what method of distribution is utilized, it is important to realize the potential consequences of each method.

Who Gets Grandma's Yellow Pie Plate?™ Workbook

Different Methods and Things to Consider

Methods of Distribution	Things to Consider...
Wills A will goes into effect when a person dies. It directs your personal representative to carry out your wishes. Listing one's personal property in a will can result in pages of detail if every item is listed. When writing a will, owners are encouraged to prepare a "separate writing identifying bequest of tangible property" as described in the next section, "Lists."	• Require, to insure accuracy, that the actual will be updated as changes in ownership or transfer wishes occur. • Frequently use vague wording such as "divide evenly among the children," thus leaving the actual decision of who gets what personal property up to the family or personal representative.
Lists Many states recognize lists, mentioned in a will, as a legal method to distribute non-titled property. A list such as this must be either in the hand-writing of the owner or signed by the owner. Property and people mentioned in the list must be clearly identified (for example, my cousin, Chris A. Anderson, the cut-glass bowl with the bird design, and so on). Lists may be prepared either before or after the will is written. Lists designating distribution of non-titled property need to be kept with personal papers, so the personal representative is able to distribute items to the intended recipients. (See Worksheet 8 for an example of how to prepare a list and a template to create a list of your own.)	• Must be mentioned in the will to be legally valid in many states. • Can provide written documentation of the owner's wishes. • May be prepared by the owner after receiving input from potential recipients. • Need to be dated to insure it represents the most recent wishes of the property owner. • Can be easily updated. • Share the list with those involved so they know your plans. Children may be more willing to accept decisions if they hear about them from you.

Different Methods and Things to Consider (cont.)

Methods of Distribution	Things to Consider...
Gifts Property may be transferred to others by gifting it prior to death. While these gifts frequently take place at birthdays and holidays, they may occur at any time. One grandmother chose to give her grandson's fiancée a crystal bowl as a shower gift. She included a note explaining that originally the bowl was received as a gift when she and her husband were married 50 years earlier. Gifts of up to $10,000 ($20,000 for married couples), or property equal to that amount, may be gifted annually without paying gift tax. Gifts may also be given to charities or museums. Check with the director or curator before gifting to these entities. Remember, once given, gifts are the permanent property of the receiver.	• Allow you to pass on stories and special memories associated with specific items. • May be given with the assumption they will be returned to the original giver. Not everyone gives gifts they would like to have returned. This assumption may make it difficult to compensate those who gave gifts such as money, clothes, or food. • Reduce the size of your estate and possibly the taxes on it. • May require filing of gift tax forms if amount exceeds limit. • May provide you with tax deductions when gifts are made to non-profit groups. Check with your tax advisor. • Provide for permanent transfer of property. Once a gift is given, it is no longer yours.
Verbal or "Someday" Promises A "someday you will receive this item" promise assumes the recipient will receive an item of property at a future point in time. For example, "After I die, I want you to have my wedding ring."	• May cause misunderstandings when more than one person feels they have been promised the same item. • May cause problems when items break, are sold or lost, or are given to another person before "someday" arrives.

Different Methods and Things to Consider (cont.)

Methods of Distribution	Things to Consider...
Labeling Items Many people place masking tape or other labels on items to identify who should receive them. Labels are not a legally valid method of transfer.	• May fall off, be removed, or become illegible. • Are not legally binding unless a valid list is also prepared.
Private Auctions Family members buy items in open bidding. Families who choose this method may use real money or "funny money," such as marbles, poker chips or play money. If real money is used, the money generated will go to the owner or to the estate and may be subject to taxes. If funny money is used, each qualified bidder receives an equal number of units for bidding.	• Allow special items to stay in the family and, thus, preserve memories. • May enable wealthier bidders to "outbid" others when real money is used. Hurt feelings and damaged relationships may result. • Allow everyone to have equal purchasing power if "funny money" is used. • Allow income to go to the estate or to the property owner if s/he is still living. • Allow the family to maintain control and privacy.
Silent Auctions with Family Family members place written bids on items. High bidder gets the item. Money goes to the estate and may be subject to taxes.	• Allow more privacy in bidding. • Allow quiet, less assertive people equal opportunity for securing items they want.

Different Methods and Things to Consider (cont.)

Methods of Distribution	Things to Consider...
Public Auctions Family members and the public bid for items. Proceeds from the auction will go to the owner or to the estate. Proceeds may be subject to taxes.	• Allow items of sentimental value to go to individuals outside the family. • May require that fees or a percentage of the sale be paid to the auctioneer. • Doesn't maintain family privacy.
Garage/Yard Sales A public sale of this type works well to distribute items of little emotional or financial value. Proceeds go to the owner or the estate and may be subject to taxes.	• May require disposal of unsold items. • May present a challenge to arrive at a "fair market value." • Doesn't maintain family privacy.
Estate Sales Property is sold to a liquidator and the money goes to the owner or the estate. Proceeds may be subject to taxes.	• May require that fees or a percentage of the sale be paid to the liquidator. • Allow items of sentimental value to transfer to people outside the family. • Doesn't maintain family privacy.
Pilfer Items When others aren't looking, heirs quietly remove items of special value.	• Can cause hurt feelings and anger which may last for years and for generations. • May be contradictory to wishes of the owner. • Means secrets are kept. This can be damaging to relationships.

Different Methods and Things to Consider (cont.)

Methods of Distribution	Things to Consider...
Family Distribution Many families choose to distribute property privately within the family. When this is done, distribution may take place item by item, or items may be placed in groups of approximately equal monetary value and then selected as a group. Here are methods which have been used by families to determine the order of selection: • Shake dice: Family members shake dice with the high roller receiving first choice, and so on. After the first round the selection order is reversed. After two rounds, family members shake again to determine a new order. • Draw numbers, straws, or playing cards. • Birth order preference: Selection goes from the oldest to youngest, or vice versa. • Gender preference: Selection begins with males before females, or vice versa. Birth order may also be integrated into this method. • Generation preference: Priority is given to parents, siblings, children, grandchildren, or blood kin.	• Allows the family to maintain control and privacy. • May give all family members equal chance to receive prized items. • Needs to recognize the difficulty of placing a dollar value on emotionally cherished items. • Is often utilized immediately following a death while family members are still in the grieving process. This may be extremely difficult for some. • Requires family members to be physically present to make decisions. • May not reflect the property owner's wishes. • May not enable the stories to be passed on with the items if it occurs after the owner's death. • May choose to emphasize differences in family status. • May make it difficult for everyone to agree on how to determine a value (financial or emotional) for items.

Different Methods and Things to Consider (cont.)

Methods of Distribution	Things to Consider...
Removal of Leftover/Unclaimed Property One or more family members assume responsibility for removing all remaining property, going through it item by item to insure that valuable items aren't discarded. (One family almost discarded a patent for a disposable baby bottle that had been granted to their mother.)	• Once items are disposed of, they are gone forever. Items that may not seem to have value today, may be more appreciated tomorrow or next year.
Throwing Away While it may be necessary for some property to be discarded, property owners are encouraged to consider donating items to such non-profits as the Salvation Army or a women's shelter. Environmentally appropriate practices are also encouraged.	• May adversely affect the environment. • Donating items to non-profit groups may qualify you or the estate for a tax benefit. Consult your tax advisor.
Intestate Transfers — Dying Without a Will If you own property at the time of your death, and have not made a will, the state, through intestate succession laws, dictates how your titled and non-titled property will be distributed. Although states differ, there is a planned, legal succession of levels of heirs documented in each state's statutes.	• Gives equal amounts to heirs at the same level (that is, siblings) regardless of the owner's wishes or intentions. • Does not allow for any special bequests.

If You Do Nothing: One Example of Intestate Succession

When a person dies without a will, decisions about who gets what are usually governed by state inheritance law. Family members may be surprised or upset when they find that these decisions are outside of their control. If you live in Minnesota, for example, you may or may not be aware of the following details of state inheritance law:

- The surviving spouse inherits all when there are no children.

- If the living children are all children of both spouses, the surviving spouse inherits all.

- When the deceased has children with a previous spouse, the current spouse will share the estate with step-children.

- Without a surviving spouse, all children divide the estate equally.

- Without a spouse or children, grandchildren or other heirs are sought.

Decisions legally rest with the property owner while alive.

Worksheet 8 List Identifying Transfer Wishes

Many states recognize lists, mentioned in a will, as a legal method to distribute non-titled property. Lists may be prepared either before or after the will is written.

Depending on inheritance law in your state, the property owner may be able to complete the following list and mention the list in her or his will, and to heirs. A list such as this must be either in the handwriting of the owner or signed by the owner. Property and people mentioned in the will must be clearly identified. Should the owner wish to make any changes to the list, he or she must make and sign a new list.

Here is an example of a separate list that identifies the transfer wishes of a property owner (for distribution of personal property according to Minnesota Statutes, Section 524.2-513).

Page _____ of _____

To: My Family, Heirs, Executor or Personal Representative

This is the list that I referred to in my Last Will and Testament. Therefore, please distribute the items listed below to the persons I have named:

Item	To Be Distributed To
Grandfather's clock (from the living room)	My sister, Susan Anderson Jones
Grandfather's woodworking tools (from the basement)	My brother, George J. Anderson
My collection of flower vases	My sister Susan's son, Bill A. Jones

My Signature (Testator): _____ Date: _____

Directions: Consult an attorney or other source to determine how the laws in your state govern the transfer of non-titled property. If a list is allowed, complete the following page of this worksheet to identify your transfer wishes. If a list is not allowed in your state, it still may be helpful to complete the list to better prepare yourself for getting your transfer wishes organized and formalized.

This worksheet was written by Marlene S. Stum, University of Minnesota Extension and Department of Family Social Science.

© 2011, Regents of the University of Minnesota. All rights reserved.

In accordance with the Americans with Disabilities Act, this worksheet is available in alternative formats upon request. Direct requests to 1-800-876-8636.

University of Minnesota Extension is an equal opportunity educator and employer.

Visit us online at www.yellowpieplate.umn.edu.

Worksheet 8: List Identifying Transfer Wishes (cont.)

To: My Family, Heirs, Executor or Personal Representative   Page _____ of ـ_____

This is the list that I referred to in my Last Will and Testament. Therefore, please distribute the items listed below to the persons I have named:

Item	To Be Distributed To
_____	_____
_____	_____
_____	_____
_____	_____
_____	_____
_____	_____
_____	_____
_____	_____
_____	_____
_____	_____
_____	_____
_____	_____
_____	_____
_____	_____
_____	_____
_____	_____

My Signature (Testator):_____ Date: _____

What Did You Learn?

Which method(s) of distribution will work best for your family or for your situation?

Are there others with whom you should discuss options?

> ### ▶ Next Step
>
> Once you have decided on the method of distribution that best fits your situation, it is important for the participants to agree on ground rules for the process. Continue on to "Chapter 7: Determine Distribution Options and Establish Ground Rules," in which distribution ground rules are discussed.

Notes:

Chapter 7: Determine Distribution Options and Establish Ground Rules

by Claire Althoff, University of Minnesota Extension

I am overwhelmingly sad. When Mom died, my three older sisters took it upon themselves to divide up Mom's dishes and household items. They assumed that, as a guy, I wouldn't want any of these things. At the time, I didn't object. I was used to having them boss me around.

Now I have two beautiful daughters who will never have a special remembrance from their grandmother. I wish I had something of Mom's to give my daughters.

Who should get to make the rules? What would have happened if I had stood up to them?

— Tim

Agree on a Process

Transferring non-titled personal property—such as Grandma's yellow pie plate and Uncle Harry's gold watch—will take time as well as physical and emotional energy. When families begin the distribution process, there are sure to be different assumptions, questions, and opinions on how the process should be handled. Establishing ground rules prior to beginning distribution may help the process go more smoothly. The following suggestions can help your family begin this process, ideally before a death occurs.

Considering Ground Rules

Suggestions	Things to Consider...
Plan carefully where you will meet.	• Is the location large enough to accommodate the number of people who will be involved in the process? Will young children be present or will other arrangements be made for childcare? • Will the location hinder or encourage open discussion of feelings and ideas? • Does the location accommodate health restrictions and physical comfort of the people who will be there (that is, "smoke free" for those with allergies; handicap accessible for those with limitations on mobility; access to food, restrooms, and space to stretch)?
Think before selecting a time for distribution. The distribution process may be a stressful time for families. Often families begin this process shortly after a funeral or crisis. Depending on family circumstances and places of residence, you may want to consider delaying the property distribution temporarily.	• What is the best time for family members to convene for property distribution? When is the least stressful time to distribute the property?
Decide property owner's role in discussions and decisions.	• Making decisions prior to death or other crisis, allows property owners to ask others for input.

Considering Ground Rules (cont.)

Suggestions	Things to Consider...
Decide children/grandchildren/ relatives' role in discussions and decisions.	• Will children/grandchildren be given preference based on age, gender, or other factors? • Will adopted, step, or foster children be involved in the discussions? • How will children/grandchildren from distant locations be included?
Decide personal representative(s)/ executor/executrix's role in discussions and decisions.	• Will the personal representative accept input from others?
Decide in-laws' role in discussions and decisions.	• Will children's spouses (in-laws) be included in the distribution? Will the couple be viewed as "one" or "two?" • Does including in-laws make the group too large? • What skills (mediation, clearer perspectives) might in-laws add to the group?
Decide friends/significant others/ partners/ex-spouses' role in discussions and decisions.	• Are there close friends who should be included in the process?
Decide caregiver's role in discussion and decisions.	Are there caregivers—either family members or others—who have had a significant role in the life of the property owner?

Considering Ground Rules (cont.)

Suggestions	Things to Consider...
Decide attorneys/legal representative's role in discussion and decisions.	• Are there attorneys named who should legally be involved? • Should legal representatives be involved in decision-making? Will additional fees be charged for having their involvement?
Decide mediator's role in discussions and decisions.	• Does the family need help defining common goals and keeping discussions focused from someone trained in mediation? • Would it be beneficial for a professional mediator to serve as a neutral third party to help keep discussions orderly, fair, and focused?
Discuss and determine goals. Individuals may have varying goals for the distribution process. Discuss individual goals and identify group priorities. Focusing on common goals may help reduce conflict.	• Use the worksheets available in this workbook to identify goals. See "Chapter 3: Determine What You Want to Accomplish."
Determine a process for resolving conflicts before they occur.	• Will the group look for a simple majority when settling differences or will the group try to find a compromise that is tolerable for everyone? See "Chapter 8: Managing Conflicts if they Arise."

Considering Ground Rules (cont.)

Suggestions	Things to Consider...
Recognize differences. Some people make decisions very quickly, while others need more time to process information. Some people make significant sacrifices in order to prevent damage to relationships, while others thrive on having power over people, regardless of the cost to the relationships.	• Determine how different personalities and decision styles can be blended to negotiate compromises.
Designate a recorder. This person should record decisions accurately. Individuals involved with the process should "sign off" on agreements at the conclusion of the distribution.	• By having people sign off on the agreement, you may eliminate the problem of people coming back at a later time to disagree on the way property was distributed. Decide as a group when, or if, negotiations may be re-opened.
Pay attention to basic stress management strategies. Distributing non-titled property may cause stress in the lives of those involved. Be aware of signs of stress such as irritability, overwhelming sadness, explosive arguments, back pain, high blood pressure, and disturbed sleep patterns.	• Get physical exercise. Remember your mind and body work together. Exercise will help you release pressure when you are angry, nervous, or upset. • Get plenty of rest. Property distribution is hard work. Lack of sleep can quickly make people irritable and/or overly sensitive. Adequate rest may help alleviate this problem.

Considering Ground Rules (cont.)

Suggestions	Things to Consider...
Pay attention to basic stress management strategies. (cont.)	• Consider making a "no alcohol and drugs" rule. Self-medication and alcohol may add additional stress to an already tense situation. As a family you know your situation best and may want to consider this option. • Establish a schedule. Distribution takes time. Set up meeting dates and times, both starting and ending. Be sure to plan for "think" time, "cool down" time, and breaks. • Balance nutritious eating with the need for "comfort foods."

What Did You Learn?

Take time now to summarize the decisions you have made about the process that will work best for you and your family. Write the details below.

Where and when will we meet?

Who will participate?

Who will act as a recorder?

What are the goals?

What methods will we use to manage conflicts if they arise?

What will we do to minimize stress?

Other considerations:

▶ Next Step

The process of passing on personal possessions can be emotional and involve conflict. "Chapter 8: Managing Conflicts if they Arise" will help you understand that disagreements are normal and can be handled so that the outcome is positive.

Notes:

Chapter 8: Managing Conflicts if they Arise

by Christy Bubolz, University of Minnesota Extension

There are six daughters in my family. The three oldest each had their own baptismal gown, while my younger sisters and I all shared one gown.

After Mom died, my sister Connie (second youngest) was pretty upset about which of us younger girls would get the gown, or how we'd share it and who would decide. Every sister had a different opinion, and some of the discussions got pretty heated.

Finally, Ann suggested the younger sisters draw straws for three special items: the shared baptismal gown, the First Communion dress worn by all six of us, and Mom's wedding dress. It turned out to be a great solution.

— Liz

Disagreements and conflicts in families are normal—in the course of everyday life, and also during the emotional process of transferring personal property.

While no one single communication strategy will insure you are going to "get your own way," the following suggestions may help work through differences and conflicts if they arise. Improving communication can help family members deal more effectively with the problems and issues related to transferring non-titled property. Ideas on improving communication, listening, speaking, and working on conflicts follow.

Just Listen

Listen before you try to figure out what to say. Listening is the part of communication we often forget. While we are worrying about what to say, we may miss what the other person said, meant, and felt. Meanwhile, that person may be doing the same. Listening doesn't mean agreeing! You can listen to others without adopting their ideas or agreeing with them.

Listening can give family members the message you respect and care about their ideas and thoughts. Listening for the content, meanings, and feelings behind the words will give you a much better understanding of others and their thoughts.

Emotions are expressed in face and body language.

Listening helps others more fully express their thoughts and feelings. When they know they are being heard and respected, individuals can, in turn, become better listeners.

Tips for Better Listening

To be a better listener, think about how you behave while someone is talking. Try to hear the meanings and feelings behind the words.

To be a better listener:

- Recognize that listening takes a lot of energy and cannot be maintained for long time periods. Set your limits—fifteen minutes, a half an hour, or whatever works well for you.

- Shut out distractions such as fidgeting, TV, looking out the window, or playing with a pencil. It is harder to listen when people are paying more attention to their surroundings than to the people in the room.

- Maintain good eye contact. Look the person in the eye, but don't stare. Recognize that emotions are expressed in face and body language.

- "Square up" to the person talking. For direct communication, align your shoulders with theirs. This will help shut out other distractions.

- Lean toward the speaker. Give the message you are trying to get closer to their thoughts.

- Keep distance to a minimum. Don't talk across a room; sit or stand a comfortable distance apart.

Listen for Feelings

Emotions may run high when you are talking about the transfer of personal property. At times like these, reflective listening is important. Reflective listening brings emotions and feelings out in the open. It helps to clarify problems and keeps communication going. For reflective listening, you continue using the skills of a good listener, but you go further to catch feelings and state back to people what you think you hear them saying.

Reflective listening means paying close attention to the feelings behind the words. In reflective listening you listen for the feelings and reflect those feelings back to the person speaking in your own words. For example: "Am I right that you feel disappointed with what is going on?" or "You sound angry with Dad for dying." Reflect back your perception of what the problem is, what the feelings are, and leave an opening for the person to correct your perception.

How Do I Say What I Need to Say?

Listening is one part of good communication; speaking is the second part of the process. When you have strong feelings, it is important to express yourself so others don't take offense. Put together your thoughts and feelings about the events that are occurring.

The way you state your thoughts and feelings should be non-threatening and non-blaming. This will help others listen without taking offense and works well in emotional settings. This is often done with "I" messages.

The way you state your thoughts and feelings should be non-threatening and non-blaming.

> "Say not you know another entirely, till you have divided an inheritance with him."
>
> —Johann Kaspar Lavater, 1788

"I" messages contain these three parts, not necessarily in this order:

- State the problem, issue, or unacceptable behavior;
- Describe your feelings as a result of the behavior; and
- Express the effect of the behavior.

Here are examples of "I" statements:

- "Dad, since Mom has been ill and we started talking about moving you to an apartment in town, I've been worried about how decisions will be made about sorting through all your things. I've tried to bring this up before, and I'm concerned that if we don't talk about this soon, Mom won't be able to participate in making the decisions."

- "Molly, I was at Mother's house yesterday, and I noticed that her curio cabinet is empty. I'm upset that you may have taken her doll collection without discussing it with me. It's been so hard on both of us since she died, and I need to know I can trust you and talk to you about how we divide up her things."

- "Uncle Leo, I called to tell you how much it meant to me to be included in family discussions about what will happen to Aunt Carla's personal possessions. I was hoping I would get one of her special tapestries, but I didn't know she asked that all her needlework to go to your church. Now I understand and I'm glad you're doing what she wanted."

"I" messages take thought and practice. Just having "I" in a statement doesn't make it an "I" message if it is sending blaming messages about "you." "I" messages are personal expressions of feelings, concerns, and needs. Such messages need to be very specific and identify exact behavior and situations of concern.

Working on Conflicts

Decisions about the transfer of personal property are often frustrating because of different values and perceptions of what is "right." Many people are uncomfortable making decisions involving people when there are conflicting values or roles. This may be especially true when people have a continuing relationship. Having a conflict with a store clerk is much different than having one with a relative to whom you will be connected for the rest of your life.

Managing family conflicts includes having family members:

1 Discuss and clarify the problem.
   - Are there common goals those involved hope to accomplish in the transfer of personal property?
   - Are there common ideas about what is a fair process of transfer?
   - Are there common viewpoints about who should get what items?

2 Make a commitment to work on the problem and toward a solution.
   - Exclude personal opinions.
   - Focus on the problem or issue, not on the person talking.

When you have strong feelings, it is important to express yourself so others don't take offense.

Decisions about the transfer of personal property are often frustrating because of different values and perceptions of what is right.

- Listen for the feelings behind the words spoken.
- Think before speaking.
- Respect the views of others.
- Bring feelings out into the open.

3 State personal needs.

- Use "I" statements to convey your feelings and needs. Take responsibility for yourself.

4 Consider alternatives, select a solution, and evaluate the choices.

- What goals are the most important? Which of the alternatives being considered will promote your common goals? Selecting an alternative is not the end. You may want to reevaluate the choice as you work with it. New information may surface that will make another alternative a better fit with the priorities of family members.

Can You Agree to Disagree?

Even when those involved don't agree, they can still show respect for the opinions and decisions of others. Remember that different ideas about what's fair regarding personal property transfer should be expected. While families can work through sensitive issues on their own, some may benefit from a professional mediator. A mediator can provide an impartial, more objective perspective. Certified mediators can be found in the yellow pages under "Mediation Services." They are trained to provide a process or method to help you reach a decision.

Watch for Blaming

One barrier to setting aside personal feelings and dealing with the problem at hand is blaming. Blaming may occur when family members struggle to deal with the difficult situation of the death of a loved family member and the need to disperse memory-laden objects at the same time. Blaming is an attempt to find a reason or a scapegoat. Blaming may be viewed as a problem because it oversimplifies the situation and makes people into "good guys" and "bad guys."

Here are examples of blaming messages:

- "If you didn't invite the in-laws into this discussion, we wouldn't be fighting."

- "You think just because you're the oldest, you get to make all the decisions."

- "What makes you think you get the photographs? Mom promised them to me!"

Blaming often stands directly in the way of moving forward. While it is a natural emotion and reaction, it doesn't help solve problems. When transfer decisions are made during a family crisis, people can be more inclined to blame others. Individuals are also more likely to blame themselves and others during the anger and depression stages of the grief cycle.

"If only" does not help solve problems. Since family members may be at different stages of the grief process, it is easy to think that others don't care about your feelings or that others aren't trying hard enough to handle the situation. It is easy to blame family members who feel differently than you do.

Blaming can be reduced by:

- Being supportive and understanding of the feelings of others;

- Letting family members know if you feel blamed;

- Expressing your feelings at the situation, not at the individuals; and

- Talking about what is happening and how you feel.

Remember Your Reasons for Completing this Process

If, at times, this process becomes frustrating, return to "Worksheet 1: "Understanding Why You Are Completing this Workbook." Doing so will remind you and others of the importance of your work. You may also have realized additional reasons and goals that will help you move forward.

> ### Next Step

> Now it is time to communicate decisions to others, and to take steps to be sure legal documents are completed that will ensure your wishes, or the wishes of others, can be carried out as intended. That is the subject of "Chapter 9: Planning is a Process."

Notes:

Chapter 9: Planning is a Process

by Marlene S. Stum, University of Minnesota Extension and
Department of Family Social Science

> I had a minor stroke last year and it really got me thinking. My husband, Corky, died four years ago, and we never talked about what would happen to our belongings. He inherited everything from his parents because he was the oldest, but his brother never spoke to him again.
>
> I couldn't stand the thought of that happening with my kids, so at a family dinner I brought up the subject. We started talking about what was fair, agreed to meet again, and now those decisions have all been made. I've made a list of who should get what, and now I'm ready to meet with my attorney to update my will. I'm relieved that my children won't fight about this after I'm gone.
>
> — Joy

Where Are You in the Planning Process?

If you are finishing this workbook, congratulate yourself and any others who have helped. You have done the work necessary to make important decisions that many people overlook.

Most people (six out of ten) haven't completed either a will or a process for transferring their personal property. Even those who have a will often include only vague directions such as "divide my personal property equally among my children." This type of language provides little practical direction to family and friends dealing with complex emotions and relationships. When these decisions are made prior to death, research shows that family and friends are more likely to accept the outcome, and there are fewer misunderstandings about the property owner's wishes. Family, friends and future generations will also benefit from the special memories and stories that have been shared.

Remember, transferring property is a process. If you haven't completed transfer decisions review the following pages of this workbook for more direction. Your completion steps will vary depending on your role in the process, and the timing of your work.

Who Gets Grandma's Yellow Pie Plate?™ Workbook

Planning is a Process 85

When transfer decisions are made prior to death, family and friends are more likely to accept the outcome.

If you are a:

- Property owner, refer to page 87;

- Child or other potential receiver working with a parent or property owner who is living, refer to pages 88-89;

- Child or other potential receiver dealing with the belongings of a parent or property owner who has died, refer to pages 90;

- Personal representative (executor/executrix) working with a property owner who is living, refer to pages 91-92;

- Personal representative (executor/executrix) dealing with the belongings of a property owner who has died, refer to page 93.

✔ Completion Steps: Property Owners

After property transfer decisions have been made, property owners may need to:

- **Ensure that inheritance documents are legally in order.** This workbook is not intended as a substitute for legal guidance. Because inheritance laws differ from state to state, it is important that you have sound legal information and advice.

  One way to do this is to seek the advice of an attorney with expertise in estate planning and inheritance law. Another is to contact your local Bar Association, Legal Aid Society, or county legal assistance office. These organizations offer information and legal assistance at reduced rates to those who are otherwise unable to afford it.

- **Communicate wishes and decisions to others.** Doing so personally will help reduce misunderstandings and give you an opportunity to discuss how and why you made the decisions you did. You may choose to have such discussions with immediate family members, your personal representative or others who may need to know this information. For tips on talking about sensitive issues, see "Chapter 2: Understanding the Sensitivity of Transferring Personal Property," and "Chapter 8: Managing Conflicts if they Arise."

- **Begin gifting.** If you select gifting as a distribution method, you may want to begin giving those treasured belongings as gifts at holidays, birthdays or other occasions.

- **Tell the stories.** Now is the time to share stories about the personal history associated with your special treasures. You may do this in writing, or by recording in audio or video. Tell others why certain objects have meaning for you, and, when appropriate, why you have decided to pass these objects on to them.

- **As your family and possessions change, revisit and update your decisions.**

✔ Completion Steps: Children and Others Working with a Property Owner

If the parent or property owner has not given specific instructions about how personal possessions are to be distributed, children or other potential receivers may need to:

- **Work on bringing up the topic.** See the sections in Chapter 2 entitled "Beginning the Process," "Reasons Given for Avoiding the Issue," and "Tips on Talking About Sensitive Issues."

- **Work with any personal representative the property owner may have designated.** If the property owner has named someone to act as a personal representative (such as an estate executor or executrix), that person will need to be included in decision-making—both for legal reasons and out of respect for the wishes of the property owner.

- **Help the property owner sort out goals.** See "Chapter 3: Determine What You Want to Accomplish."

- **Encourage discussion about fairness.** See "Chapter 4: Determine What Fair Means."

- **Talk with the property owner about the objects that are important to you, and those you think might be meaningful to others; encourage identification of special objects.** See "Chapter 5: Identify Special Objects to Transfer."

- **Help the property owner to understand distribution options.** See "Chapter 6: Distribution Options and Consequences."

- **Help the property owner select a process for transferring property.** See "Chapter 7: Determine Distribution Options and Establish Ground Rules."

- **Help manage conflicts.** See "Chapter 8: Managing Conflicts if they Arise."

After property transfer decisions have been made, you may need to:

- **Help the property owner ensure that inheritance documents are legally in order.** This workbook is not intended as a substitute for legal guidance. Because inheritance laws differ from state to state, it is important that property owners have sound legal information and advice.

- One way to do this is to seek the advice of an attorney with expertise in estate planning and inheritance law. Another is to contact your local Bar Association, Legal Aid Society, or county legal assistance office. These organizations offer information and legal assistance at reduced rates to those who are otherwise unable to afford it.

- **Encourage the property owner to communicate wishes and decisions to others.** When property owners do this personally, they reduce misunderstandings and provide an opportunity to discuss how and why decisions were made. Property owners may choose to have such discussions with immediate family members, their personal representatives or others who may need to know this information. For tips on talking about sensitive issues, see "Chapter 2: Understanding the Sensitivity of Transferring Personal Property," and "Chapter 8: Managing Conflicts if they Arise."

- **Encourage the property owner to begin gifting.** If the property owner selects gifting as a distribution method, he or she may want to begin giving treasured belongings as gifts at holidays, birthdays or other occasions.

- **Encourage the property owner to tell her or his stories.** Now is the time for property owners to share stories about the personal history associated with their special treasures. This can be done in writing, or recorded in audio or video. Encourage them to tell others why certain objects have meaning, and, when appropriate, why they have chosen certain people to receive them.

- **As family and possessions change, encourage the property owner to revisit and update his or her decisions.**

- **Begin making decisions now about your own non-titled property.**

✔ Completion Steps: Children and Others Dealing with the Belongings

If the parent or property owner has not given specific property transfer instructions, children or other potential receivers may need to:

- **Work with any personal representative the property owner has designated.** If the property owner has named someone to act as a personal representative (such as an estate executor or executrix), that person will need to be included in decision-making—both for legal reasons and out of respect for the wishes of the property owner.

- **Work on bringing up the topic with surviving family members and other potential receivers of property.** See the sections in Chapter 2 entitled "Beginning the Process," "Reasons Given for Avoiding the Issue," and "Tips on Talking About Sensitive Issues."

- **Identify individual and group goals.** See "Chapter 3: Determine What You Want to Accomplish."

- **Encourage discussion about fairness.** See "Chapter 4: Determine What Fair Means."

- **Encourage family members and other potential property receivers to talk about the objects that are important to them, and those they think might be meaningful to others; identify special objects.** See "Chapter 5: Identify Special Objects to Transfer."

- **Determine what distribution options will work best for your situation.** See "Chapter 6: Distribution Options and Consequences."

- **Help select a process for transferring property.** See "Chapter 7: Determine Distribution Options and Establish Ground Rules."

- **Help manage conflicts.** See "Chapter 8: Managing Conflicts if they Arise."

After property transfer decisions have been made, you may need to:

- **Communicate decisions to others.** For tips on talking about sensitive issues, see "Chapter 2: Understanding the Sensitivity of Transferring Personal Property," and "Chapter 8: Managing Conflicts if they Arise."

- **Begin making decisions now about your own non-titled property.**

✔ Completion Steps: Personal Representatives Working with a Property

If the property owner has not given specific instructions about how personal possessions are to be distributed, personal representatives (executors/executrixes) may need to:

- **Work on bringing up the topic with the property owner.** See the sections in Chapter 2 entitled "Beginning the Process," "Reasons Given for Avoiding the Issue," and "Tips on Talking About Sensitive Issues."

- **Work with any family members or friends the property owner wishes to include in decision-making.**

- **Help the property owner sort out goals.** See "Chapter 3: Determine What You Want to Accomplish."

- **Encourage discussion about fairness.** See "Chapter 4: Determine What Fair Means."

- **Encourage the property owner to identify special objects.** See "Chapter 5: Identify Special Objects to Transfer."

- **Help the property owner select distribution options.** See "Chapter 6: Distribution Options and Consequences."

- **Help the property owner select a process for transferring property.** See "Chapter 7: Determine Distribution Options: Establish Ground Rules."

- **Help manage conflicts**. See "Chapter 8: Managing Conflicts if they Arise."

After property transfer decisions have been made, you may need to:

- **Help the property owner ensure that inheritance documents are legally in order.** This workbook is not intended as a substitute for legal guidance. Because inheritance laws differ from state to state, it is important that property owners have sound legal information and advice.

One way to do this is to seek the advice of an attorney with expertise in estate planning and inheritance law. Another is to contact your local Bar Association, Legal Aid Society, or county legal assistance office. These organizations offer information and legal assistance at reduced rates to those who are otherwise unable to afford it.

- **Encourage the property owner to communicate wishes and decisions to others.** When property owners do this personally, they reduce misunderstandings and provide an opportunity to discuss how and why decisions were made. Property owners may choose to have such discussions with immediate family members, their personal representatives, or others who may need to know this information. For tips on talking about sensitive issues, see "Chapter 2: Understanding the Sensitivity of Transferring Personal Property," and "Chapter 8: Managing Conflicts if they Arise."

- **Encourage the property owner to begin gifting.** If the property owner selects gifting as a distribution method, she or he may want to begin giving treasured belongings as gifts at holidays, birthdays or other occasions.

- **Encourage the property owner to tell his or her stories.** Now is the time for property owners to share stories about the personal history associated with their special treasures. This can be done in writing, or recorded in audio or video. Encourage them to tell others why certain objects have meaning, and, when appropriate, why they have chosen certain people to receive them.

- **As family and possessions change, encourage the property owner to revisit and update his or her decisions.**

- **Begin making decisions now about your own non-titled property.**

✔ Completion Steps: Personal Representatives Dealing with the Belongings

If the property owner has not given specific instructions about how personal possessions are to be distributed, personal representatives may need to:

- **Work with any family members or friends the property owner wished to include in decision-making.**

- **Work on bringing up the topic with family members or other potential property receivers.** See the sections in Chapter 2 entitled "Beginning the Process, "Reasons Given for Avoiding the Issue," and "Tips on Talking About Sensitive Issues."

- **Help family members and other potential receivers sort out goals.** See "Chapter 3: Determine What You Want to Accomplish."

- **Encourage discussion about fairness.** See "Chapter 4: Determine What Fair Means."

- **Encourage family members and other potential property receivers to talk about the objects that are important to them, and those they think might be meaningful to others; encourage identification of special objects.** See "Chapter 5: Identify Special Objects to Transfer."

- **Help select distribution options.** See "Chapter 6: Distribution Options and Consequences."

- **Help select a process for transferring property.** See "Chapter 7: Determine Distribution Options and Establish Ground Rules."

- **Help manage conflicts.** Recognize it is primarily your responsibility to be sure the owners wishes are followed. See "Chapter 8: Managing Conflicts if they Arise."

After property transfer decisions have been made, you may need to:

- **Communicate decisions to others.** For tips on talking about sensitive issues, see "Chapter 2: Understanding the Sensitivity of Transferring Personal Property," and "Chapter 8: Managing Conflicts if they Arise."

- **Begin making decisions now about your own non-titled property.**

Notes:

Appendix A: Glossary

Appraisal: A value judgment about economic worth made in writing by someone with expertise to do so. Such an expert, called an appraiser, can be found in the yellow pages under "Appraisers."

Assumption: A fact or statement believed to be true.

Communication: Exchange of information or messages in any way, such as by talking, writing, or gestures.

Conflict: Opposition of people or values.

Decision-making process: The process of determining solutions to problems including goal setting, consideration of options, and consequences.

Decision: A determination arrived at after consideration.

Distribution options: Specific methods or choices for transferring personal property either before or after death.

Emotional value: Personal memories or feelings attached to material items which provide meaning or sentiment not easily measured in economic value.

Entitlement: Something one has a right to.

Equal: A fairness rule in which the emphasis is on treating everyone the same.

Equitable: A fairness rule whereby individual differences in needs, contributions, or status are used as the basis for distribution.

Estate: The accumulation of one's property, including both titled and non-titled property, making up one's net worth.

Estate planning: A process involving the accumulation, preservation, use, and distribution of one's property before and after death.

Executor: The person appointed by a testator to execute one's will.

Executrix: A female executor.

Expectations: What one anticipates or assume will happen or take place.

Fairness: Perception of what rules should be used to allocate or transfer non-titled property in a just manner.

Family history: A record or recollection of events transmitted or shared from one generation to another.

Family legacies: Property and stories handed down from previous generations.

Family traditions: Family rituals, customs, or practices repeated over time which provide meaning and memories for participants.

Feelings: A person's emotional perceptions in reaction to specific events, objects, and places.

Gifting: The act of giving property to others prior to death; provides for permanent transfer of property or financial assets.

Goal: A statement of what one wants to accomplish.

"Grandma's Yellow Pie Plate": A metaphor or figure of speech referring to non-titled personal property. Non-titled property typically has emotional value as well as potential economic value.

Grieving: The process of dealing with grief and loss over time.

Ground rules: Specific arrangements, procedures, or methods which all participants agree to follow.

"I" statements: The person speaking states his or her viewpoint, desire, belief, or intention without sending blaming messages to the listener(s).

Inheritance: Property transferred to an heir after one's death; anything received from an estate.

Intestate transfers: How the state distributes one's titled and non-titled property if one dies without a will.

Legal representative: A person legally named to make decisions for another, for example, one having Durable Power of Attorney, or a Personal Representative.

Lottery system: A distribution system whereby persons have equal chance to receive a specific object.

Meaning: The significance or interpretation attached to specific objects or events.

Mediator: An outside party who can facilitate a process to focus discussions and reach outcomes. Professional mediators have specific expertise acquired through training and skills. Professional mediators are frequently attached to dispute centers or agencies dealing with conciliation. Consult the yellow pages under "Mediators."

Non-titled property: Personal property without a legal document (title) to indicate who officially owns the item. These items may or may not have great financial value, but often have a great deal of sentimental or emotional value.

Objects: Items that can be seen or touched.

Outcomes: Results, or who gets what, in property transfers.

Perceptions: Viewpoints or understandings individuals hold.

Personal belongings/property: Material possessions that have no legal title, for example furniture, clothing, tools, and dishes.

Personal representative: Person responsible for carrying out one's wishes; may be legally designated, as in a will, or appointed by the court.

Potential receiver: Individual who may be receiving personal property when transfer takes place.

Proceeds: The sum or profit derived from a sale.

Role: A function or position assumed by someone.

Sensitivity: Awareness or recognition of how emotions affect communication.

Sentimental value: The worth of an object that comes from memories, emotions, and feelings.

Testator: A person who leaves a will or testament in force upon death.

Title: A legal document to indicate who owns the item, for example, real estate, vehicles, or financial assets.

Titled property: Property with a legal title or document to indicate who officially owns the items (such as real estate, savings accounts, or vehicles with title).

Transfer: The process of moving ownership of property from one person to another.

Transfer goals: Determination of what one wants to accomplish when ownership of personal property is moved from one person to another.

Transitions: Changes.

Unfair: Perception of injustice or that the "rules" have been violated by family members.

Unwritten rules: Methods or procedures understood or accepted as true.

Will: A legal document written to control what happens to property and assets when one dies. A will may also direct guardianships for dependent children, including minors.

Appendix B: References

Abrahms, S. (2010, September 20). Oh Brother! With parents aging, squabbling siblings turn to elder mediation. *AARP Bulletin*. Retrieved from:
www.aarp.org/relationships/family/info-09-2010/elder_mediation.html

Allianz. (2005, October 19). *Research finds huge "legacy gaps" in boomers and parents' views of inheritance*. Minneapolis, MN: Allianz Life Insurance Company of North America.

Angel, J. L. (2007). *Inheritance in contemporary America: The social dimensions of giving across generations*. Balitmore, MD: John Hopkins University Press.

Cates, J. N., & Sussman, M. B. (Eds.). (1982). Family systems and inheritance patterns. *Marriage and Family Review*, *5*(3). New York: The Hawthorn Press.

Cohen, R. L. (1987). Distributive justice: Theory and research. *Social Justice Research*, *1*, 19-40.

Drake, D. G., & Lawrence, J. A. (2000). Equality and distributions of inheritance in families. *Social Justice Research*, *13*, 271-290.

Deutsch, M. (1985). *Distributive justice*. New Haven, CT: Yale University Press.

Ekerdt, D. J., & Sergeant, J. F. (2006). Family things: Attending the household disbandment of older adults. *Journal of Aging Studies*, *20*, 193-205.

Ekerdt, D., Sergeant, J., Dingel, M., & Bowen, M. (2004). Household disbandment in later life. *Journal of Gerontology*, *59B*, S265-S273.

Finch, J., & Mason, T. (2000). *Passing on: Kinship and inheritance in England*. London: Routledge.

Folger, R., & Greenberg, G. (1985). Procedural justice: An interpretive analysis of personnel systems. In K. M. Rowland and G. R. Ferris (Eds.), *Research in personnel and human resources management: A research annual* (pp. 141-183). Greenwich, CT: Elsevier Science Ltd.

Goodnow, J., & J. Lawrence. (2008). How should people act in inheritance situations? Specifying differences in expectations. *International Journal of Behavioral Development, 32*(2), 98-107.

Goodnow, J., & J. Lawrence. (2008). Inheritance events: Perceptions of actions that involve the giving and receiving of things. *Forum: Qualitative Social Research, 9*(1). Retrieved from www.qualitative-research.net/index.php/fqs/article/view/332

Leyenthal, G. S., Kurza. J., & Fry, W. R. (1980). Beyond fairness: A theory of allocation preferences. In G. Mikula (Ed.), *Justice and Social Interaction* (pp. 167-218). New York: Springer-Verlag.

Marx, J., Solomon, J., & Miller, L. (2004). Gift wrapping ourselves: The final gift exchange. *Journal of Gerontology, 59B*(5), S274-S280.

Price, L., Arnould, E., & Curasi, C. (2000). Older consumers' disposition of special possessions. *The Journal of Consumer Research, 27*(2), 179-201.

Reis, H. T. (1984). The multidimensionality of justice. In R. Folger (Ed.), *The Sense of Injustice: Social Psychological Perspectives*. New York: Plenum.

Rettig, K. D. (1993). Problem-solving and decision-making processes of families: An ecological framework for integrating family relations and family resource management. *Marriage and Family Review, 18*, 187-222.

Sousa, L, Silva, A., Santos, L., & Patrao, M. (2010). The family inheritance process: Motivations and patterns and interaction. *European Journal of Ageing, 7*, 5-15.

Stum, M. (2000). Families and inheritance decisions: Examining non-titled property transfers. *Journal of Family and Economic Issues*, *21*(2), 177-202.

Stum, M. (1999). I just want to be fair: Interpersonal justice in intergenerational transfers of non-titled property. *Family Relations*, *48*, 159-166.

Sussman. M. B., Cates, J. N., & Smith, D. T. (1970). *The Family and Inheritance*. New York: Sage.

Tayler, J. E., & Norris, J. E. (2000). Sibling relationships, fairness, and conflict over transfer of the farm. *Family Relations*, *49*, 277-283.

Titus, S. L., Rosenblatt, P C., & Anderson, R. M. (1979). Family conflict over inheritance of property. *The Family Coordinator*, 337-346.

Tyler, T. R. (1987). Procedural justice research. *Social Justice Research*, *1*(1), 41-66.

Appendix C: Credits

Project Development Team

All members of the original project development team are with the University of Minnesota. Six team members are Extension Educators specializing in family resource management located in counties across Minnesota. One team member is an "Extension Specialist" located on the St. Paul campus. Team members include:

- Claire J. Althoff, Wilkin County
- Shirley L. Barber, Ramsey County
- Christy A. Bubolz, Koochiching County
- Sharon S. Knutson, Norman County
- Charles F. Leifeld, Washington County
- Elizabeth H. Russell, Chippewa County
- Marlene S. Stum, Professor and Extension Specialist, Family Economics and Gerontology, Department of Family Social Science

The print materials writing sub-team included:

- Claire J. Althoff, Wilkin County
- Shirley L. Barber, Ramsey County
- Christy A. Bubolz, Koochiching County
- Sharon S. Knutson, Norman County
- Elizabeth H. Russell, Chippewa County
- Marlene S. Stum, Professor and Extension Specialist, Family Economics and Gerontology, Family Social Science
- The Watson Group, Minneapolis, Consultants

The print materials production sub-team included:

- Claire J. Althoff, Wilkin County
- Marlene S. Stum, Professor and Extension Specialist, Family Economics and Gerontology, Department of Family Social Science
- The Watson Group, Minneapolis (consultants)

Project Advisory Committee

The following individuals were involved in clarifying educational needs and approaches, identifying relevant research, and reviewing and developing written and video resources.

- Todd Andrews, Attorney, Minnesota Continuing Legal Education
- Betty Berger, Attorney, Minnesota Board on Aging
- Timothy Blade; Professor; Department of Design, Housing and Apparel; University of Minnesota
- Steve Brand; Attorney; Robins, Kaplan, Miller & Ciresi; Minneapolis, MN
- Richard Hawke, Attorney, Richard D. Hawke's private practice, Roseville, MN
- Rosalind Keppler, Attorney, Kuehn & Keppler, St. Paul, MN
- Frances Long, Attorney, Long & Collins, Minneapolis, MN
- Kris Maser; Attorney; Maser, Amundson & Crist; Minneapolis, MN
- Patricia Miller, Attorney, P.J. Miller Law Offices, St. Paul, MN
- Jane Plihal, Associate Professor, Vocational Technical Education, University of Minnesota
- Paul Rosenblatt, Professor, Department of Family Social Science, University of Minnesota
- Michael Scherschligt, School of Law, Hamline University, St. Paul, MN
- Lloyd Stern, Attorney, Hessian, McKasy & Soderberg, Minneapolis, MN
- Patti Sullivan, Attorney, Ulvin & Sulllivan, St. Paul, MN
- Mary Ward, Attorney, American Banks Trust Department, St. Paul, MN

Additional Reviewers of Written Materials for Consumers

The following people assisted in reviewing materials for this workbook:

- Sharon M. Danes, Professor and Extension Specialist, Department of Family Social Science, University of Minnesota

- Daniel F. Detzner, Associate Professor, Department of Family Social Science, University of Minnesota

- Florence Guse, Department of Public Health, Otter Tail County, Fergus Falls, MN

- Karla Krueger, Central Minnesota Council on Aging, St. Cloud, MN

- Adell Mehta, Senior Community Services, Minnetonka, MN

- Susan S. Meyers, Extension Family Sociologist, University of Minnesota Extension

- Roberta Ouse, Partners Program, Rothsay, MN

- Deborah Pankow, Family Economics Specialist, North Dakota State University

- Lorraine Patton, Mid-Minnesota Area Agency on Aging, Willmar, MN

- Kathryn K. Rettig, Professor, Family Social Science, University of Minnesota

- Danica Robson, NW Area Agency on Aging, Thief River Falls, MN

- Simone M. Sandberg, Attorney, Kragness & Sandberg Ltd., Wahpeton, ND

- Virginia Smith, West Central Area Agency on Aging, Fergus Falls, MN

- Susan St. Claire, Attorney, Susan St. Claire Law Office, International Falls, MN

Special Thanks

We would also like to thank:

- Hamline University School of Law
- University of Minnesota Law School
- William Mitchell College of Law

Funding and Financial Support

Funding and financial support for this project was provided by:

- University of Minnesota Extension (Creative Grant; Educational Materials Development Grant, Director's Office; and Financial and Business Management Specialization)
- Department of Family Social Science, University of Minnesota
- University of Minnesota Extension county offices located in:
  - Chippewa County
  - Koochiching County
  - Norman County
  - Ramsey County
  - Washington County
  - Wilkin County

Notes: